Write to Know Series

Upper Elementary

Nonfiction Writing Prompts for

Science

$$C_6H_{12}O_6$$

- Michelle Le Patner, M. Ed. - Farid N. Matuk, M.F.A.
- Rosemary Ruthven, M.S., Literacy Specialist
- Edited by Amy M. Whited, M.A.

LEAD+
LEARN
PRESS

LEAD+
LEARN
PRESS

The Leadership and Learning Center
317 Inverness Way South, Suite 150
Englewood, CO 80112
Phone 866.399.6019 or 303.504.9312 | Fax 303.504.9417
www.LeadandLearn.com

ISBN-13: 978-1-933196-05-3   ISBN-10: 1-933196-05-X

Printed in the United States of America

16 15 14 13 12   04 05 06 07 08 09

CONTENTS

Why nonfiction prompts?

Giving students reasons to write across the curriculum is one of the most powerful and time-saving strategies in the educator's toolkit. The content areas present numerous opportunities for students to engage in writing for authentic purposes; in turn, writing is an excellent vehicle for students to demonstrate their understandings of the essential concepts being taught in a content area. These prompts have been written for teachers who are committed to standards-based instruction and to integrating their curriculum. They were selected to complement (History/Social Studies/Science/Math) units of study and to give students practice in all four domains of writing.

How do I use them?

Teachers may choose to use the prompts in a variety of ways:

- As *writing-process* assignments, wherein students have several weeks to synthesize and apply essential understandings of new concepts to a quality piece of writing.
- For teacher-guided *interactive* writing lessons, during which teachers can reinforce content-area learning while also assisting students to refine their writing techniques.
- As *performance assessments,* wherein students demonstrate they can effectively answer essential questions generated from a unit of study in a content area.
- In some cases, as a *quick-write* pretest to assess students' preexisting knowledge before commencement of a unit.

When not to use them

Although some prompts could be given as quick-write assessments of students' preexisting knowledge, these prompts should be given primarily during or upon completion of a unit of study. They are not designed to be given "cold" as a test instrument to assess student writing proficiency. Clearly, if these prompts are given prior to instruction, students' writing scores will potentially be undermined by their inability to support their ideas with relevant facts and details.

Why is the wording so sophisticated?

You will note that the wording used in the prompts often mirrors that found in the standards themselves. Such terminology will be intimidating to students only if there are no strong learning associations with the meaning of the words. Kindergartners have no problems remembering what a *Tyrannosaurus rex* is; with sound instruction, nor do they have difficulty understanding terms such as *evaporation.*

Some prompts don't exactly fit the content I taught

These prompts are suggestions and a place to start. Teachers are encouraged to modify the wording of these prompts, or write their own prompts, to better fit the emphasis of the unit and the purpose of the writing. For example, they may wish to vary the number of paragraphs required, depending on what part of the year the unit was completed. They may feel that students would do better responding to the prompt in the form of a poem or a letter rather than a straight composition. Keep two important things in mind, however: students need practice in all four domains of writing, and the content taught must be standards-based.

What should I consider when writing my own prompts or when modifying existing prompts?

The wording of a prompt can either motivate or intimidate a writer. Good prompts make it very clear to students what you are asking of them. Compare the following two prompts:

1. *Explain precipitation and evaporation in at least two paragraphs.*

2. *Your friend doesn't know how there is always enough water stored in the sky to fall as rain. She also doesn't know how puddles on the playground can just disappear after a while. Write a report of at least two paragraphs to help your friend understand precipitation and evaporation.*

Prompts like the first one tend to reinforce a student's notion that writing is what one does to pass a test or complete an assignment for a grade. By contrast, the second prompt takes the following points into consideration:

- The audience for whom the student is writing is clear (a friend).

- The purpose of the writing has been specified (to help the friend understand).

- The type of writing required is referred to as a "report," reminding students that this piece of writing should be presented as straightforward prose and will not be, for example, in a letter, poem, or story format.

- The minimum number of paragraphs/sentences required has been specified.

- Some clues have been put into the prompt by way of the scenario to assist students in activating their existing knowledge on the subject.

Some other things to consider when writing prompts:

- If you are creating the prompt specifically to assess student knowledge about a content area at the end of a unit of study, design the prompt around the essential question(s) you began with at the start of the unit.

- Don't ask students to talk about anything personal that may be seen as an invasion of privacy.

- Avoid asking students to write specifically about holidays (e.g., Halloween, Christmas) or birthdays. These can be sensitive areas for some students and their parents because of religious beliefs or negative feelings about holidays.

- Be sure you could effectively write to the prompt yourself. Plan out what you would do, as an expert writer, to satisfy the requirements of the prompt.

- Write prompts that will give students practice in all four domains of writing.

What are the four domains of writing students need to practice, and why is it important for teachers to know what they are?

We use the *sensory/descriptive* domain when we write down our deepest feelings in a diary or use our five senses to describe an unusual sea creature for a scientific journal. We enjoy *imaginative/narrative* writing every time we read a novel, watch a television drama, or catch a movie. When we fill out forms, make to-do lists, summarize documents, or write directions, we are using the *practical/informative* domain. We dive into the *analytical/expository* domain when we write a campaign speech, justify an opinion, or e-mail friends convincing them to go to the holiday destination of our choosing.

The majority of writing we do in life falls under the *practical/informative* and *analytical/expository* domains—but at times those domains will contain elements of the other two. For example, a report on the results of an experiment will be more effective if it contains good sensory description; a historical novel can be a source of practical information while also being an imaginative narrative. Hence, it is vital for students to receive instruction and practice in *all four* domains. Moreover, it is crucial for students and teachers to know that although a piece may contain several elements spanning more than one domain, ultimately it is categorized by its *primary* objective. The following table gives definitions and examples of each domain.

The Domain	Its Primary Objective	Some Examples
Sensory/Descriptive	To describe an object, a moment in time, or feelings experienced in vivid, sensory detail.	■ Detailed recordings of observations made of a fossil ■ A poem describing feelings experienced after suffering an injustice ■ A character sketch of Abraham Lincoln
Imaginative/Narrative	To tell what happened in a logical sequence. This could be a real-life or imaginary series of events.	■ The autobiography of Thomas Edison ■ The story of Charlie Crawley, who started out as a caterpillar and ended up as a butterfly ■ A comic strip portraying Newton's discovery of gravity
Practical/Informative	To present basic information with clarity.	■ A business letter to the supplier of the canteen milk cartons informing them of leaks ■ Step-by step instructions for performing an experiment ■ A summary of a *National Geographic* article
Analytical/Expository	To explain, analyze, compare and contrast, or persuade.	■ A television commercial persuading viewers to recycle their soda cans ■ An explanation of the impact of the Gold Rush on life choices made by Chinese immigrants ■ A comparison of sedimentary and igneous rocks

What kind of scoring guide should I use to evaluate proficiency?

Whatever scoring guide or rubric you decide to use, ensure that the *students* know the criteria being used to assess proficiency. Those criteria may be embodied in an existing scoring guide or one you and the students have created together around the demands of a specific prompt.

Decide what you are *primarily* evaluating. Are you mainly trying to determine whether students have internalized information and acquired essential understandings, or are you evaluating *how well* they are able to use language to express what they know? Ultimately, of course, your objective is to develop proficiency in both. Certainly, if a prompt were given as a writing-process assignment to be completed over several weeks, you should reasonably expect *both* excellent content and excellent written expression to be evident. If, however, the prompt is given as a posttest at the conclusion of a unit, you may choose not to heavily penalize mistakes in sentence structure and conventions, as long as students demonstrate essential understanding(s) of the content. If you are more concerned with a student's ability to state and justify an opinion in a quick-write assignment, you may choose on that occasion not to heavily penalize inaccurate information.

The following are samples of an analytic scoring guide and a holistic scoring guide. An *analytic scoring* guide allows you to assess a student's writing proficiency trait by trait. Simply give a 1, 2, 3, or 4 score for each trait; a "3" score indicates proficiency in that area. An analytic scoring guide enables teachers to focus their instruction on those areas of writing in which a student is not yet proficient. In other words, the assessment informs instruction. The *holistic scoring guide,* in contrast, is less specific and gives the student a score based on the teacher's overall impression of the piece. As with the analytic scoring guide, a "3" is considered a proficient score.

Lower Elementary Analytic Scoring Guide

TRAIT	4 Exceeds Grade-Level Expectations	3 Proficient	2 Approaching Proficiency	1 Not Proficient
Essential understandings of content	Demonstrates essential understanding(s). Supporting details/ideas go beyond the obvious or predictable.	Demonstrates essential understanding(s). Supporting details/ideas may at times be too general or out of balance with the main idea.	Essential understanding(s) not clearly demonstrated, although an attempt was made to address the main idea.	The ideas are unclear and lack a central link to essential understanding(s).
Organization	Uses an organizational structure that fits the purpose of the writing task. Uses an inviting introduction and conclusion. Demonstrates a logical sequence of ideas.	Uses an organizational structure that fits the purpose of the writing task. Uses an introduction and conclusion. Demonstrates a logical sequence of ideas.	Uses an organizational structure that does not fit the purpose of the writing task. Attempts to write an introduction and/or conclusion. May or may not use a logical sequence of ideas.	Organizational structure is not appropriate for the purpose. No apparent beginning or conclusion. No logical sequence of ideas.

TRAIT	4 Exceeds Grade-Level Expectations	3 Proficient	2 Approaching Proficiency	1 Not Proficient
Vocabulary	Demonstrates understanding of vocabulary related to content. Uses words in an interesting, precise, and natural way appropriate to audience and purpose.	Demonstrates understanding of vocabulary related to content. Uses words in a functional way appropriate to audience and purpose.	Content vocabulary words are attempted but not applied appropriately. Words used are generally imprecise and at times may not be appropriate to audience and purpose.	Words are limited, monotonous, and/or misused. Only the most general kind of message is communicated.
Voice	Demonstrates strong audience awareness, and there is a sense of a person and a purpose behind the words. An appropriate voice or tone is *consistently* employed.	Demonstrates some audience awareness, and at times there is a sense of person and purpose behind the words. An appropriate voice or tone may not be *consistently* employed.	Demonstrates limited audience awareness; there is little sense of the person and purpose behind the words.	Shows no audience awareness; it is hard to sense the person and purpose behind the words.

TRAIT	4 **Exceeds Grade-Level Expectations**	3 **Proficient**	2 **Approaching Proficiency**	1 **Not Proficient**
Sentence fluency	Uses complete sentences with correct word order, subject/verb agreement, no run-ons or fragments. Employs correct tense and uses pronouns correctly. Varies sentence structure, length, and beginnings to strengthen the meaning of the text.	Uses complete sentences. Occasional errors in word order, tense, pronoun usage, subject/verb agreement, or use of run-ons and fragments, but errors do not detract from meaning. Varies sentence-structure length and beginnings.	May use both incomplete and complete sentences. Frequent errors in word order, pronoun usage, tense, subject/verb agreement, and/or use of run-ons and fragments; errors detract from meaning.	Uses incomplete sentences. Sentence structure may obscure meaning.

TRAIT	4 **Exceeds Grade-Level Expectations**	3 **Proficient**	2 **Approaching Proficiency**	1 **Not Proficient**
Conventions	Uses correct capitalization, punctuation, and spelling with only occasional errors. Writes with correct grammar and usage that guide the reader through the text.	Uses correct capitalization and punctuation with occasional errors. Most grade-level words are spelled correctly. Makes occasional errors in grammar and usage.	Makes capitalization and punctuation errors. There are many spelling errors that distract the reader. Errors in grammar and usage interfere with readability and meaning.	Uses random or incorrect capitalization and punctuation. Spelling errors and errors in grammar and usage block the meaning of the writing.

Student Name: _____ Date: _____

Lower Elementary Holistic Scoring Guide

4—Exceeds Grade-Level Expectations

- Demonstrates essential understanding(s) about the content and gives strong supporting details.

- Uses an organizational structure that fits the writing task, including an inviting introduction and conclusion, and demonstrates a logical sequence of ideas.

- Demonstrates understanding of content vocabulary and uses words in a natural and precise way.

- Demonstrates audience awareness; *consistently* employs an appropriate tone.

- Occasional errors (if any) in syntax, spelling, capitalization, and punctuation do not detract from meaning.

3—Proficient

- Demonstrates essential understanding(s) about the content. Supporting details and ideas may at times be too general or out of balance with the main idea.

- Uses an organizational structure that fits the writing task, including an introduction and conclusion, and demonstrates a logical sequence of ideas.

- Demonstrates understanding of vocabulary related to content and uses words in a functional way to convey message.

- Demonstrates audience awareness. May not *consistently* employ an appropriate tone.

- Errors in syntax, spelling, capitalization, and punctuation do not interfere with meaning.

2—Approaching Proficiency

- Attempts to address the main idea, but does *not* demonstrate essential understanding(s) about the content.

- Uses an organizational structure that does not fit the writing task. May use an introduction or conclusion. Sequence of ideas may not be evident.

- Content vocabulary words are attempted but not applied appropriately. Words used are generally imprecise and may not be appropriate to purpose.

- Shows limited audience awareness.

- May use both incomplete and complete sentences. Frequent errors in syntax, spelling, capitalization, and punctuation interfere with meaning.

1—Not Proficient

- The ideas are unclear and lack a central link to essential understanding(s).

- Organizational structure is not appropriate for the purpose. No apparent beginning or conclusion. No logical sequence of ideas.

- Words are limited, monotonous, and/or misused. Only the most general kind of message is communicated.

- Shows no audience awareness; it is hard to sense the person and purpose behind the words.

- Uses incomplete sentences. Errors in spelling, capitalization, and punctuation obscure meaning.

Upper Elementary Analytic Scoring Guide

TRAIT	4 **Exceeds Grade-Level Expectations**	3 **Proficient**	2 **Approaching Proficiency**	1 **Not Proficient**
Essential understandings of content	Clearly demonstrates essential understanding(s). Provides strong, credible support of the topic and shares insights that go beyond the obvious and predictable. Maintains a consistent point of view.	Demonstrates essential understanding(s). Supporting details and ideas may at times be too general or out of balance with the main idea. Maintains a mostly consistent point of view.	Essential understanding(s) not clearly demonstrated, although an attempt was made to address the main idea. Attempts are made to support ideas, but may be irrelevant. Inconsistent point of view.	Ideas are unclear and lack a central link to essential understanding(s).

NONFICTION WRITING FOR SCIENCE

TRAIT	4 **Exceeds Grade-Level Expectations**	3 **Proficient**	2 **Approaching Proficiency**	1 **Not Proficient**
Organization	Uses an organizational structure that fits the purpose of the writing task. Constructs inviting introductions and satisfying conclusions. Selects effective transitions and employs purposeful pacing.	Uses an organizational structure that fits the purpose of the writing task. Creates clear introductions and conclusions. Uses adequate transitions. Pacing may be inconsistent.	Uses an organizational structure that addresses only parts of the writing task. Undeveloped beginnings and/or conclusions and weak or overused transitions. Little knowledge of pacing.	Uses an organizational structure that addresses only one part of the writing task. No apparent beginning or conclusion.

TRAIT	4 **Exceeds Grade-Level Expectations**	3 **Proficient**	2 **Approaching Proficiency**	1 **Not Proficient**
Vocabulary	Demonstrates understanding of vocabulary related to content. Uses fresh and lively expressions that at times include figurative language or slang.	Demonstrates understanding of vocabulary related to content. Uses words in an interesting, precise, and natural way appropriate to audience and purpose.	Content vocabulary words are attempted but not applied appropriately. Words used are generally imprecise and at times may not be appropriate to audience and purpose.	Words are limited, monotonous, and/or misused. Only the most general kind of message is communicated.

TRAIT	4 **Exceeds Grade-Level Expectations**	3 **Proficient**	2 **Approaching Proficiency**	1 **Not Proficient**
Voice	Demonstrates strong audience awareness; there is a sense of a person and a purpose behind the words. An appropriate voice or tone is consistently employed. Topic is brought to life through conviction, excitement, or humor.	Demonstrates audience awareness; there is a sense of a person and a purpose behind the words. An appropriate voice or tone is employed most of the time.	Demonstrates limited audience awareness; there is little sense of the person and purpose behind the words. Uses a voice that is overly informal or impersonal and flat.	Shows no audience awareness. It is hard to sense the person and purpose behind the words. Voice is consistently flat.

TRAIT	4 **Exceeds Grade-Level Expectations**	3 **Proficient**	2 **Approaching Proficiency**	1 **Not Proficient**
Sentence fluency	Uses complete sentences with correct word order, subject/verb agreement, no run-ons or fragments. Employs correct tense and uses pronouns correctly. Varies sentence structure, length, and beginnings to strengthen the meaning of the text.	Uses complete sentences. Occasional errors in word order, tense, pronoun usage, subject/verb agreement, or use of run-ons and fragments, but errors do not detract from meaning. Varies sentence-structure length and beginnings.	May use both incomplete and complete sentences. Frequent errors in word order, pronoun usage, tense, subject/verb agreement, and/or use of run-ons and fragments; errors detract from meaning.	Uses incomplete sentences. Sentence structure may obscure meaning.

TRAIT	4 **Exceeds Grade-Level Expectations**	3 **Proficient**	2 **Approaching Proficiency**	1 **Not Proficient**
Conventions	Uses correct capitalization and punctuation. Uses correct spelling of even the most difficult grade-level words. Writes with correct grammar and usage that guide the reader through the text. Consistently uses paragraph breaks that reinforce organization and meaning.	Uses correct capitalization and punctuation. Most grade-level words are spelled correctly. Makes occasional errors in grammar and usage. Employs paragraph breaks that generally reinforce organization and meaning.	Makes capitalization and punctuation errors. Frequent spelling errors distract the reader. Errors in grammar and usage interfere with readability and meaning. Paragraph breaks (if any) may be irregular and bear little relation to the organization of the text.	Uses random or incorrect capitalization and punctuation. Spelling errors and errors in grammar and usage block the meaning of the writing.

Student Name: _____ Date: _____

Upper Elementary Holistic Scoring Guide

4—Exceeds Grade-Level Expectations

- Demonstrates essential understanding(s) about the content and gives supporting details that go beyond the predictable. Maintains a consistent point of view.

- Uses an organizational structure that fits the purpose of the writing task. Constructs inviting introductions and satisfying conclusions. Consistently uses paragraph breaks that reinforce organization and meaning.

- Selects effective transitions and employs purposeful pacing.

- Demonstrates understanding of vocabulary related to content. Uses fresh and lively expressions that at times include figurative language or slang.

- Demonstrates a strong audience awareness; there is a sense of a person and a purpose behind the words. Consistently employs an appropriate voice or tone. Topic is brought to life through conviction, excitement, or humor.

- Only occasional errors (if any) in syntax, spelling, capitalization, and punctuation. Writes with correct grammar and usage that guide the reader through the text.

3—Proficient

- Demonstrates essential understanding(s) about the content. Supporting details and ideas may at times be too general or out of balance with the main idea. Maintains a mostly consistent point of view.

- Uses an organizational structure that fits the purpose of the writing task. Creates clear introductions and conclusions. Employs paragraph breaks that generally reinforce organization and meaning. Uses adequate transitions. Pacing may be inconsistent.

- Demonstrates understanding of vocabulary related to content. Uses words in an interesting, precise, and natural way appropriate to audience and purpose.

- Demonstrates audience awareness; there is a sense of a person and purpose behind the words. Employs an appropriate voice or tone most of the time.

- May be some syntax, spelling, capitalization, and punctuation errors, but they do not interfere with meaning.

2—Approaching Proficiency

- Attempts to address the main idea, but does not demonstrate essential understanding(s) about the content.

- Uses an organizational structure that does not fit the writing task. May use an introduction or conclusion. Sequence of ideas may not be evident.

- Content vocabulary words are attempted but not applied appropriately. Words used are generally imprecise and at times may not be appropriate to audience and purpose.

- Demonstrates limited audience awareness; there is little sense of a person and purpose behind the words. Uses a voice that is overly informal or impersonal and flat.

- May use both incomplete and complete sentences. Frequent errors in syntax, spelling, capitalization, and punctuation detract from meaning.

1—Not Proficient

- Ideas are unclear and lack a central link to essential understanding(s).

- Organizational structure is not appropriate for the purpose. No apparent beginning or conclusion. No logical sequence of ideas.

- Words are limited, monotonous, and/or misused. Only the most general kind of message is communicated.

- Shows no audience awareness; it is hard to sense a person and purpose behind the words.

- Uses incomplete sentences; errors in spelling, capitalization, and punctuation obscure meaning.

Effective assessment is the foundation of effective accountability.

—Douglas B. Reeves, Ph.D. (2004, p. 17)

       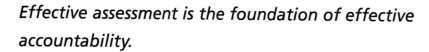 $C_6H_{12}O_6$

We know that some creatures, like lizards, need to absorb energy from the sun by lying out under its light and heat. Write a poem describing what it is like to be a lizard, a snake, or some other reptile that needs to receive and store heat energy during the day so that it can be active at night. Describe what it feels like to lie motionless for so long under the hot sun inside your rough skin. Imagine what you see walking by as you lie there, and describe how it feels as the heat is converted to energy for you.

    $C_6H_{12}O_6$

An effective accountability system must answer at least four common sense questions: one about individual student achievement; a second about school performance; a third about ways to help students learn; and a fourth about determining educational effectiveness.

—Douglas B. Reeves, Ph.D. (2004, p. 26)

$C_6H_{12}O_6$

Imagine that you were turned into a snowman while you slept. You know the sun will soon come out and start melting and evaporating your body. Write a story about how you survived the day without melting and evaporating. Be sure to use science words such as *solid*, *liquid*, and *gas*.

    C₆H₁₂O₆

Students should never have to wander aimlessly through their educational journeys, wondering what they need to do in order to please the teacher.

—Douglas B. Reeves, Ph.D. (2004, p. 33)

        $C_6H_{12}O_6$

How would you feed an alien that is hungry for energy? Imagine that one of these creatures has come to visit your classroom and will be happy to eat energy in any of its forms. Write a set of instructions for the alien, listing all the sources of stored energy in your classroom and telling him how to access them. Remember that you're a source of stored energy too, so be careful not to get yourself eaten!

C₆H₁₂O₆

As a matter of fairness and good educational practice, students deserve to have their work evaluated against an objective standard.

—Douglas B. Reeves, Ph.D. (2004, p. 34)

 34

        $C_6H_{12}O_6$

An ancient scientist, Dr. I. M. Smart, needs your help. He believes that all matter is made up of earth, wind, fire, or water. Write him a letter very respectfully telling him that he is mistaken. Explain that more than 100 different types of atoms have been discovered and that these are represented in the periodic table. Help him understand by discussing what happens to water when it is heated and evaporates.

35

    $C_6H_{12}O_6$

Students need frequent feedback about their performances compared with clear, objective standards—not as compared with the performance of their peers.

—Douglas B. Reeves, Ph.D. (2004, p. 38)

        C₆H₁₂O₆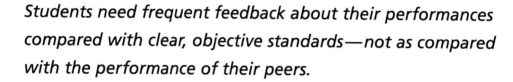

NONFICTION WRITING FOR SCIENCE

We know that light is reflected from mirrors and other surfaces. Try reflecting the light from a flashlight or the sun in one direction or another with a small mirror. Then write down your observations. Describe what you saw when the light hit the mirror and when you moved the mirror. Where did the light go? Describe it in such a way that you paint a picture in the reader's mind.

SCIENCE—PHYSICAL SCIENCES

   $C_6H_{12}O_6$

SENSORY/DESCRIPTIVE

The purpose of accountability is to improve student achievement.

—Douglas B. Reeves, Ph.D. (2004, p. 41)

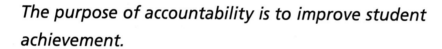

A fable is a story with a message. For example, "The Hare and the Tortoise" teaches us that it is important to pace yourself. The story of "The Lion and the Mouse" reminds us that kindness to even the smallest of creatures is significant.

You are going to write a fable that shows it is important to consider others' feelings.

Imagine that the inhabitants of a small village have been rehearsing daily for six months to put on a shadow puppet performance. Without warning, Madam Sun went into hiding behind the clouds for some reason. The show couldn't go on without her help, so the Moon decided to pay her a visit. He discovered that Madam Sun's feelings had been hurt by the villagers taking her kindness to them for granted. Once the Moon had discovered the problem, he and the villagers found a solution. Now it is your turn to make the fable come to life.

    $C_6H_{12}O_6$

Teacher assessment gives a more comprehensive view of student performance than a single test score.

—Douglas B. Reeves, Ph.D. (2004, p. 55)

NONFICTION WRITING FOR SCIENCE

In learning about light and reflection, you have done many experiments. List the steps of your favorite experiment with light so that someone in your family or one of your friends can recreate it.

    $C_6H_{12}O_6$

PRACTICAL/INFORMATIVE

Accountability systems that fail to recognize the importance of teaching ... will fail to achieve their primary objective: the improvement of student learning.

—Douglas B. Reeves, Ph.D. (2004, p. 58)

         $C_6H_{12}O_6$

NONFICTION WRITING FOR SCIENCE

Your friend from the Midwest visited the ocean for the first time and doesn't understand why on some days it looked gray-green and on other days it looked blue. Is someone painting the ocean? We know that the color of light striking an object changes the way the object is seen. Use your knowledge to explain what is happening to make the ocean's water appear to change color.

      $C_6H_{12}O_6$

In response to the diverse needs of its students, a school district must be committed to maintaining equity and must set high standards and expectations for all students.

—Douglas B. Reeves, Ph.D. (2004, p. 94)

         $C_6H_{12}O_6$

NONFICTION WRITING FOR SCIENCE

We know that magnets have two poles (north and south), and that like poles repel each other and unlike poles attract each other. Imagine that you and a friend are magnetic, wearing helmets of unlike poles. What is it like to walk around together? Is it comfortable? Be sure to describe what happens and how it feels.

Writing is a process, not a product.

—Douglas B. Reeves, Ph.D. (2002, p. 61)

         $C_6H_{12}O_6$

Imagine that you have two dogs that are always fighting, making loud noises, and disturbing the whole neighborhood. Luckily, you know that like magnetic poles repel each other. Write a story about how you used your knowledge of magnetic poles to keep these two dogs apart. Remember to describe the problem and how you thought of the solution.

     C₆H₁₂O₆

$C_6H_{12}O_6$

SCIENCE—PHYSICAL SCIENCES

IMAGINATIVE/NARRATIVE

47

Qualities of Effective Feedback: Specificity, Consistency, Accuracy

—Douglas B. Reeves, Ph.D. (2002, pp. 67–70)

Your friend the explorer is lost. From his boat he's sent a message in a bottle asking for your help. Write him a set of instructions on how to make a simple compass. You will put the instructions in a bottle and send the bottle back to him on the next tide.

Extension: Students might also include instructions on how to use the compass in relation to a map.

    $C_6H_{12}O_6$

PRACTICAL/INFORMATIVE

Scoring guides can encourage the discouraged student and challenge the complacent student.

—Douglas B. Reeves, Ph.D. (2002, p. 75)

50

NONFICTION WRITING FOR SCIENCE

We know that electrical energy can be converted to heat, light, and motion, but it isn't always easy to explain how this happens to younger children. Choose one of these conversions and write a simple explanation of how it works and why the resulting energy is so useful. Then, choose a child from a grade or two below yours and help him or her understand the concept.

ANALYTICAL/EXPOSITORY

There are three types of analytical writing: parts of a whole, cause and effect, and similarities and differences.

—Douglas B. Reeves, Ph.D. (2002, p. 89)

52

       $C_6H_{12}O_6$

We know that all matter is made of atoms, which may combine to form molecules. We also know that scientists have developed instruments that can create discrete images of atoms and molecules, which show that atoms and molecules often occur in well-ordered arrays. Write a poem describing the arrays of the following substances: sugar ($C_6H_{12}O_6$), water (H_2O), helium (He), oxygen (O_2), nitrogen (N_2), and carbon dioxide (CO_2).

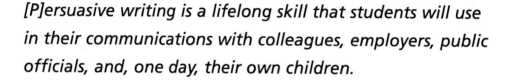

[P]ersuasive writing is a lifelong skill that students will use in their communications with colleagues, employers, public officials, and, one day, their own children.

—Douglas B. Reeves, Ph.D. (2002, p. 98)

 54

         $C_6H_{12}O_6$

We know that during chemical reactions the molecules in the reactions rearrange to form products with different properties. You are water (H_2O). Write a ballad that narrates how your molecules react and rearrange as you go from one physical state to another (solid, liquid, gas).

    $C_6H_{12}O_6$

SCIENCE—PHYSICAL SCIENCES

IMAGINATIVE/NARRATIVE

Persuasive Writing and PEAS—Problem, Evidence, Arguments, Solution

—Douglas B. Reeves, Ph.D. (2002, p. 99)

         $C_6H_{12}O_6$

NONFICTION WRITING FOR SCIENCE

You have learned the properties of solid, liquid, and gaseous substances. Helium (He), oxygen (O_2), nitrogen (N_2), and carbon dioxide (CO_2) are all colorless, odorless gasses, and yet they have different properties. Tell why they are different by detailing their elements and combinations.

    $C_6H_{12}O_6$

Organization is a requirement for good writing, and pre-writing is the best way to ensure that one's writing is organized in a logical and coherent manner.

—Douglas B. Reeves, Ph.D. (2002, p. 41)

58

$C_6H_{12}O_6$

You're in charge of an advertising campaign to convince everyone that aluminum is the best metal to conduct heat. Write the script for a radio commercial convincing audience members that they should not settle for metals composed of a combination of elemental materials, but should choose a metal such as aluminum with pure elements. Conclude with a slogan such as, "Remember, Al is your pal!"

    $C_6H_{12}O_6$

SCIENCE—PHYSICAL SCIENCES

ANALYTICAL/EXPOSITORY

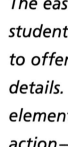

The easiest way to encourage better description from student writers is to ask questions. Although it is tempting to offer direction and instruction, only questions elicit details. Our questions should focus on both the obvious elements of description—the details of appearance and action—and on the less apparent details of emotion, feelings, thoughts and impressions.

—Douglas B. Reeves, Ph.D. (2002, p. 84)

$C_6H_{12}O_6$

We know that organisms have different physical structures for different jobs. Choose your favorite animal and describe in detail the physical structure it uses to defend itself from predators. Remember that not all animals defend themselves by tooth and nail; some use camouflage, swift legs, and noxious gas. What structure does your animal use for defense?

    $C_6H_{12}O_6$

When children are writing about their own thought processes, it is a very useful exercise for them to confront and acknowledge potential analytical errors.

—Douglas B. Reeves, Ph.D. (2002, p. 87)

62

         $C_6H_{12}O_6$

NONFICTION WRITING FOR SCIENCE

We know that changes in the environment can cause the extinction of some species and the success of others. Imagine a sudden change in our environment and choose one species that would benefit from it. Perhaps it is a weather change, a food shortage, or a major disaster. Write a story of at least three paragraphs telling how that species came to expand and dominate the planet. Remember, it might be a plant.

Students need the freedom to be original and creative and, at the same time, they need to learn how to apply standard literacy conventions.

—Douglas B. Reeves, Ph.D. (2002, p. 142)

64

      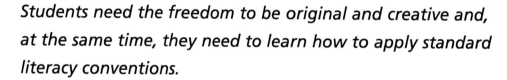   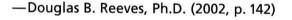

You've been hired to write a visitor's guide for your favorite environment (ocean, desert, tundra, forest, grasslands, or wetlands). Create a brochure informing visitors about the types of plants, mammals, reptiles, and insects they can expect to meet when they visit this environment. Inform them also of any precautions they should take to protect themselves or the species in that environment from harm.

Why write? Writing contributes to the creation of a sense of connection and personal efficacy by participation in society.

—Douglas B. Reeves, Ph.D. (2002, p. 30)

         C₆H₁₂O₆

NONFICTION WRITING FOR SCIENCE

You've landed on a planet with little or no oxygen and too much carbon dioxide. Luckily, you brought along a bag full of different plant seeds. Write a script of a journalist's TV interview with you answering questions about your discovery of the problem on the planet, and your ingenious solution that made the planet habitable for future human space travelers.

     $C_6H_{12}O_6$

SCIENCE—LIFE SCIENCES

PRACTICAL/INFORMATIVE

The best creative writing delights our senses, challenges our minds, and engages a broad range of emotional reactions, including love and anger, sadness and joy, contempt and empathy.

—Douglas B. Reeves, Ph.D. (2002, p. 124)

             $C_6H_{12}O_6$

Choose an extinct species you've learned about to compare with a species that is living now (e.g., dinosaurs and lizards, wooly mammoths and elephants). Explain their similarities and differences.

    $C_6H_{12}O_6$

The teachers who ask elementary students to write research papers are performing an exceptional service, provided that they help children approach the project in a carefully orchestrated, step-by-step fashion.

—Douglas B. Reeves, Ph.D. (2002, p. 105)

      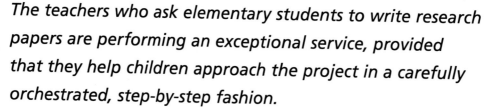 $C_6H_{12}O_6$

NONFICTION WRITING FOR SCIENCE

Fungi, insects, and microorganisms are known as
decomposers. They recycle matter from dead plants and
animals. Write a poem that describes this process.

     C₆H₁₂O₆

SENSORY/DESCRIPTIVE

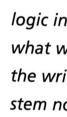

The emphasis we place on evidence, argumentation, and logic in the creation of a persuasive essay must not obscure what we know to be an essential element of great writing— the writer's passion. The best efforts of our children will stem not from our direction, but from heartfelt involvement in a subject.

—Douglas B. Reeves, Ph.D. (2002, p. 100)

72

$C_6H_{12}O_6$

NONFICTION WRITING FOR SCIENCE

Producers and consumers are related in food chains in an ecosystem. Imagine that you are a blade of grass. You are eaten by an herbivore, which is then eaten by a carnivore, which is then eaten by a decomposer. Write a narrative of at least three paragraphs to describe your transformations.

    $C_6H_{12}O_6$

We also need persuasive writing skills to protect and maintain those things we value, from a species threatened with extinction to a family tradition that is in danger of neglect. We persuade, in other words, to influence the actions and beliefs of others.

—Douglas B. Reeves, Ph.D. (2002, p. 98)

$C_6H_{12}O_6$

Many plants depend on animals for pollination and seed dispersal. Write a definition of *pollination*, briefly state why it is important to plants, and then summarize how a bird assists in pollination and seed dispersal.

    $C_6H_{12}O_6$

While students are knee-deep in the process of composing, they need feedback from both teachers and peers.

— Perchemlides and Coutant, (2004, p. 54)

          C$_6$H$_{12}$O$_6$

All organisms need energy and matter to live and grow. In turn, living organisms depend on one another and on their environment for survival. Choose an organism to research and write a composition of at least four paragraphs explaining how its environment supports its survival.

    C₆H₁₂O₆

ANALYTICAL/EXPOSITORY

In the upper elementary grades, students move from childhood to adolescence. As they continue to learn about reading and writing, they broaden and deepen their ability to use literacy as a multifaceted tool for learning. They discover their voices as writers and refine their instincts as readers.

—Fountas and Pinnell, (2001, p. vi)

$C_6H_{12}O_6$

Describe what it's like to breathe. You'll be surprised how much there is to write about if you really pay attention to your breathing. Think about how the air feels as it enters your nose and travels down into your lungs. Describe what changes in your body are visible to your eye as you inhale and exhale (look for the inflation and deflation of the diaphragm and stomach). Then describe exchanges that occur, that are not visible to the eye, as the oxygen enters the bloodstream and carbon dioxide is exhaled.

    $C_6H_{12}O_6$

The middle ground, where both reason and research are found, is that while demographic factors such as poverty and second languages are clearly associated with lower student performance, the impact of these factors is less than the impact of great teaching and school leadership.

—Douglas B. Reeves, Ph.D. (2004, p. 170)

$C_6H_{12}O_6$

NONFICTION WRITING FOR SCIENCE

Imagine that scientists have found a way to make you
and a protective observation capsule microscopic in size.
You and the capsule are injected into the bloodstream
of a living person's body. Write the story of your adventure
as you circulate through the heart chambers, lungs,
and body.

    $C_6H_{12}O_6$

SCIENCE—LIFE SCIENCES

IMAGINATIVE/NARRATIVE

Young writers need the same support structures that professional writers need, including a quiet place to work and the necessary supplies. Writing is thinking. A peaceful environment is essential for students to do their best thinking and writing.

—Fountas and Pinnell, 2001, p. 59)

NONFICTION WRITING FOR SCIENCE

Imagine that you are a digestive park ranger. You've found a piece of food that is lost and hiding between two teeth. Where should it go? Diagram and label a map to the entire digestive system so there's no danger of the food losing its way. Then write a set of instructions for the food, just to be sure!

C₆H₁₂O₆

$C_6H_{12}O_6$

SCIENCE—LIFE SCIENCES

PRACTICAL/INFORMATIVE

Feedback is effective because it shares three characteristics: specificity, consistency, and accuracy.

—Douglas B. Reeves, Ph.D. (2002, p. 76)

       $C_6H_{12}O_6$

A group of alien scientists is developing a new, human-like lifeform. They are deciding whether to give it a sequential digestive system like that of humans, or a simpler system like that of a cell, which absorbs nutrients through its outer membrane. Decide which digestive system is better, and prepare an oral presentation to convince the alien scientists that your choice is best.

    $C_6H_{12}O_6$

Because children can vary within moments across the performance continuum from novice to progressing to proficient to exemplary, parents and teachers must be ready to vary their feedback techniques appropriately.

—Douglas B. Reeves, Ph.D. (2002, p. 76)

86

       $C_6H_{12}O_6$

It's a very hot summer and all your friends would like to cool off after a long game of basketball. Because of a water shortage, the neighborhood pool isn't available, so someone suggests that everyone just get out the hose and play water games. There's some disagreement among your friends about whether this is a good idea. Prepare for a debate to argue both sides. You won't know which side of the argument you will be asked to debate, so find reasons to both support and disagree with the following statement:

Hoses are the best way to stay cool in the summer heat.

    $C_6H_{12}O_6$

SCIENCE—EARTH SCIENCES

ANALYTICAL/EXPOSITORY

Consistent encouragement [should be] not only for the final display of skill, but for each incremental step along the way.

—Douglas B. Reeves, Ph.D. (2002, pp. 69–70)

88

       C₆H₁₂O₆

Your friend has found a very small freshwater fish coming out of the tap in her bathroom, and she's very mad about it. She can't understand why the people who manage our water would put fish into the water system! Write a step-by-step report that will show her the origin of the water source for our community and how it reaches our bathrooms.

    C₆H₁₂O₆

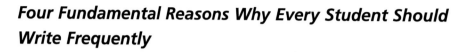

Four Fundamental Reasons Why Every Student Should Write Frequently

1. *Writing improves reading comprehension.*

2. *Writing improves student performance in other academic areas, including social studies, science, and mathematics.*

3. *Writing contributes to a sense of connection and personal efficacy by participation in society.*

4. *Writing, particularly with evaluation, editing, revision, and rewriting, will improve the ability of a student to communicate and succeed on state and local writing tests.*

—Douglas B. Reeves, Ph.D. (2002, p. 3)

        $C_6H_{12}O_6$

The moon's appearance changes during the four-week lunar cycle. Think of the last time you saw a full moon. Describe the scene for your readers in detail. Where were you? Was it cold out? What did the moon look like? What color was it? Be sure to use at least two paragraphs to show—not just tell—about your experience. Use metaphors and similes to paint a picture in the reader's mind.

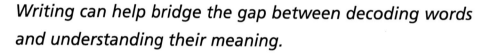

Writing can help bridge the gap between decoding words and understanding their meaning.

—Douglas B. Reeves, Ph.D. (2002, p. 4)

       C₆H₁₂O₆

Choose your favorite constellation and imagine that it moves freely about the sky. What would a night in its life be like? Write a story of at least two paragraphs telling about an adventure it has with other constellations it meets during the night.

C₆H₁₂O₆

SCIENCE—EARTH SCIENCES

IMAGINATIVE/NARRATIVE

[S]upport student writing, because it is the skill most directly related to improved scores in reading, social studies, and even mathematics.

—Douglas B. Reeves, Ph.D. (2002, p. 5)

94

$C_6H_{12}O_6$

Your friend would like to know how she might see more stars. Help her by writing out instructions for using a telescope. Should she take it out at night or during the day? Should she stay close to electric lights or go somewhere dark? Give her all the information she needs to see more stars.

$C_6H_{12}O_6$

SCIENCE—EARTH SCIENCES

PRACTICAL/INFORMATIVE

Interestingly, students who write more frequently perform better not only on essay exams or other tests that require student writing, but also on multiple-choice tests across a range of subjects.

—Douglas B. Reeves, Ph.D. (2002, p. 5)

96

       $C_6H_{12}O_6$

Imagine you have a giant alien for a friend and this giant alien is planning a vacation to our solar system just to get a good suntan. His travel agent told him the best place to be was the moon, but you disagree. Choose a better place for him to catch some solar rays, and write him a letter persuading him to come to Earth for his vacation.

    $C_6H_{12}O_6$

When students engage in frequent writing, particularly with specific feedback, editing, and revision, they are building their reasoning and thinking skills.

—Douglas B. Reeves, Ph.D. (2002, p. 5)

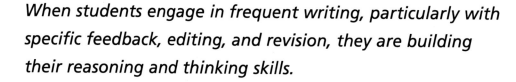

$C_6H_{12}O_6$

We know that moving water erodes landforms, reshaping the land by taking it away from some places and depositing it as pebbles, sand, silt, and mud in other places (weathering, transport, and deposition). Imagine that you are a cliff. Describe what it would be like to be beaten by waves every day. Are you eroding? What does that feel like, and is your appearance changing?

$C_6H_{12}O_6$

SENSORY/DESCRIPTIVE

*The reason for the strong relationship between writing
and test performance is unclear, but it probably relates to
the relationship between writing and thinking.*

—Douglas B. Reeves, Ph.D. (2002, p. 5)

            C$_6$H$_{12}$O$_6$

NONFICTION WRITING FOR SCIENCE

Imagine that you've been away on vacation and you come back to find that a huge, cone-shaped mountain has grown in your schoolyard. You know that such a sudden change was probably caused by a volcanic eruption. Write a narrative of at least four paragraphs telling what happened and how you and your friends learned to make room for the new volcano in your schoolyard.

$C_6H_{12}O_6$

SCIENCE—EARTH SCIENCES   IMAGINATIVE/NARRATIVE

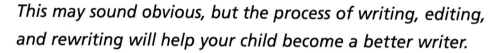

This may sound obvious, but the process of writing, editing, and rewriting will help your child become a better writer.

—Douglas B. Reeves, Ph.D. (2002, p. 7)

102

        $C_6H_{12}O_6$

Your friend has found a rock with some shiny minerals in it, but doesn't know what it is. Help her by listing directions for using a table of diagnostic properties to identify the type of mineral she has found.

    C₆H₁₂O₆

Writing is so easily avoided, and the demands for writing are so infrequent that very bright children can emerge from elementary school with good reading skills, splendid social skills, and superb academic gamesmanship, and yet face the prospect of entering their middle-school years as dreadful writers. That gap between the demands of secondary school and the meager writing skills possessed by these students will undermine their self-confidence and motivation, with detrimental impact on every subject.

—Douglas B. Reeves, Ph.D. (2002, p. 7)

104

          C₆H₁₂O₆

You and your friend are sitting on a beach while on vacation. Your friend wonders how all that sand got to the beach. After going home and learning about water erosion at school, you decide to write a letter to your friend explaining the production of sand. Remember to use scientific words like *weathering*, *transport*, and *deposition*, and be sure to explain the meaning of these words by giving examples of each.

C₆H₁₂O₆

105

They will become better writers by writing more frequently and, most important, critically reviewing their work, revising it, and getting detailed feedback from other writers, including fellow students, teachers, and parents.

—Douglas B. Reeves, Ph.D. (2002, p. 7)

106

        $C_6H_{12}O_6$

Did you know you have a mini-science experiment at home every time someone in your home boils water? Next time something is being boiled on the stove at home, observe what happens from a safe distance. Describe your observations of the water as it begins to boil, rises as steam, hits the ceiling on a cold winter's day, and forms droplets of water on surrounding cabinets. Use all of your senses and talk about what you see happening, the sounds you hear, the sensation of the humidity in the air around the boiling pot, and the transformation the water went through. Remember to keep a safe distance away from the boiling water while making your observations.

    $C_6H_{12}O_6$

Students today must write more frequently, in more different subjects, with greater sophistication, using more research, and with more accuracy than ever before.

—Douglas B. Reeves, Ph.D. (2002, p. 13)

         C₆H₁₂O₆

Imagine that you are an interstellar police officer chasing an alien criminal who is using comet transportation. The criminal has hidden somewhere in the solar system and it's your job to find him. Write a story of at least four paragraphs telling of your interplanetary adventure. Consider beginning from Earth. Describe the scenes and adventures you have on each planet until you eventually locate the criminal.

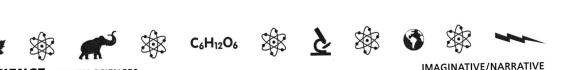

Third graders should be able to: determine the theme or an author's message in fiction and nonfiction text; demonstrate an understanding of the theme or message by writing an accurate summary of the text; use pre-writing strategies, including web, list, and outline; create a first draft, edit and revise the draft, and create a second draft; edit the work of other students, suggesting improvements and identifying errors; create single paragraphs with topic sentences and simple supporting facts and details; write descriptive pieces about people, places, things, or experiences; develop a unified main idea and use details to support the main idea; write a complete sentence of statement, command, question, or exclamation, using appropriate final punctuation; write legible in printing or in cursive.

—Douglas B. Reeves, Ph.D. (2002, p. 16)

110

$C_6H_{12}O_6$

NONFICTION WRITING FOR SCIENCE

Because she felt sick when she ate a carrot one day, your teacher thinks that all vegetables make her sick. Do you think this is a reasonable assumption? Of course not! Explain to your teacher why this is not a scientific assumption.

    $C_6H_{12}O_6$

SCIENCE—INVESTIGATION AND EXPERIMENTATION

ANALYTICAL/EXPOSITORY

Fourth graders should be able to: write informal pieces with three or more paragraphs, including an introductory paragraph, supporting paragraphs with details, and a conclusion that summarizes the essay; write paragraphs with a central idea contained in a topic sentence at or near the beginning of the paragraph; use correct indentation of paragraphs, as well as proper spelling, grammar, and punctuation; demonstrate a recognition of audience, including the use of letters, essays designed to persuade, and essays designed to give directions; create interesting sentences by using words that describe, explain, or provide additional details; identify and use adjectives and adverbs; summarize written text of approximately four hundred words by providing a legible written summary that is accurate and in order; analyze two different written texts, correctly identifying similarities and differences; write legibly in printing and in cursive; use a word processor to create a paragraph, save, print and edit a document.

—Douglas B. Reeves, Ph.D. (2002, p. 16)

 $C_6H_{12}O_6$

NONFICTION WRITING FOR SCIENCE

Knowing what you do about how different plants survive better in particular environments, you may be able to predict how a bamboo plant would react compared with a cactus plant when both are placed in the same hot, sunny place without water for one month.

Imagine you conducted this experiment for kindergarten children. Write a brief narrative describing the kindergarten setting, how the children helped you set up the experiment, and their reaction to the outcomes.

    $C_6H_{12}O_6$

Fifth graders should be able to: write informational pieces with five or more paragraphs; present important ideas or events in sequence or in chronological order; provide details in supporting paragraphs and include transitions linking paragraphs; write a research report about important ideas, issues, or events. The research paper includes a narrowly framed question that directs the research and an outline of the paper; uses a variety of information sources, including firsthand interviews, reference materials, and electronic resources; a first and second draft, and a bibliography; demonstrate an understanding of the requirements of academic integrity by complete and accurate citations of sources; identify and correctly use appropriate tense (past, present, past participle); write legibly in cursive and print; use a word processor to create a paragraph, save, print, and edit a document; create and include in a paper a chart, table, or graph in two forms: a word processed document and a hand-drawn document.

—Douglas B. Reeves, Ph.D. (2002, p. 17)

114

$C_6H_{12}O_6$

NONFICTION WRITING FOR SCIENCE

Your friend insists that scientists make up explanations about why some plants do better in certain environments than others. Define *observation* and *interpretation* for your friend and tell her how scientists use both to formulate explanations and theories.

    $C_6H_{12}O_6$

SCIENCE—INVESTIGATION AND EXPERIMENTATION

PRACTICAL/INFORMATIVE

The type of writing most closely related to the improvement of student reading skills is the creation of a clear and accurate summary of a story, article, chapter, or book that the student has read.

—Douglas B. Reeves, Ph.D. (2002, p. 21)

        $C_6H_{12}O_6$

NONFICTION WRITING FOR SCIENCE

Record the length and weight of a cactus plant and a bamboo plant. Find a way to graph your recordings. Diagram and describe the structures you observe on each plant. Place both plants in the same hot, sunny place where they won't be disturbed or watered for one month. Repeat your observations, recordings, and descriptions every week for one month.

Once you have conducted this experiment, synthesize your observations and inferences to theorize why one plant may have reacted more favorably to those conditions than the other.

    $C_6H_{12}O_6$

SCIENCE—INVESTIGATION AND EXPERIMENTATION

ANALYTICAL/EXPOSITORY

There are three intellectual skills that students develop when they write about what they have read: summarization, analysis, and prediction.

—Douglas B. Reeves, Ph.D. (2002, p. 21)

118

$C_6H_{12}O_6$

We know that water, sugar, and minerals are transported through a vascular plant. Write step-by-step instructions for an experiment to demonstrate that this is true. Following your directions, conduct the experiment and record your observations. Finally, write a report of the investigation, drawing possible conclusions and indicating whether further information is needed to support the conclusions.

    $C_6H_{12}O_6$

Provided with the opportunity to write summaries, analyses, and predictions, students will gain the confidence to consider increasingly complex text and master multiple levels of meaning. Writing improves the child's engagement with the text.

—Douglas B. Reeves, Ph.D. (2002, p. 29)

$C_6H_{12}O_6$

Write a riddle for each type of environment you've been studying. Describe it in detail without naming it and then ask the question, "What am I?" Play the riddle game with your friends and family.

   $C_6H_{12}O_6$

SENSORY/DESCRIPTIVE

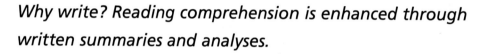

Why write? Reading comprehension is enhanced through written summaries and analyses.

—Douglas B. Reeves, Ph.D. (2002, p. 30)

122

         $C_6H_{12}O_6$

Imagine that you are the moon watching a little boy measure how much he can see of you each evening. He was very sad when he saw you disappearing until his father told him you would be a full moon again after a four-week lunar cycle. Write the story of the little boy describing how he measured your appearance each week, what he discovered, and his relief once he realized you would be your old self again.

    $C_6H_{12}O_6$

SCIENCE—INVESTIGATION AND EXPERIMENTATION   IMAGINATIVE/NARRATIVE

Why write? Writing improves student performance in other academic areas, including social studies, science, and mathematics.

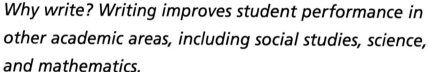

—Douglas B. Reeves, Ph.D. (2002, p. 30)

          $C_6H_{12}O_6$

Your teacher is lost somewhere in an unknown environment. Write ten questions you can ask her by phone to get a detailed description of the environment she is in so you can help her identify where she is.

     $C_6H_{12}O_6$

SCIENCE—INVESTIGATION AND EXPERIMENTATION   PRACTICAL/INFORMATIVE

Why write? Writing improves through practice, evaluation, editing, and rewriting.

—Douglas B. Reeves, Ph.D. (2002, p. 30)

          $C_6H_{12}O_6$

Your friend tells you that if you sit in front of your heater, you will get a suntan. Write down an experiment you could conduct to determine the validity of your friend's statement, and then predict the outcome. Finally, compare the result to the prediction.

    $C_6H_{12}O_6$

Bibliography

Fountas, I. C., and G. S. Pinnell. *Guiding Readers and Writers, Grades 3–6.* Portsmouth, NH: Heinemann Press, 2001.

Perchemlides, N., and C. Coutant. "Growing Beyond Grades." *Educational Leadership* 62, no. 2 (October 2004): 53–56.

Reeves, D. B. *Accountability in Action.* Englewood, CO: Advanced Learning Press, 2004.

Reeves, D. B. *Reason to Write,* Elementary School Edition. New York: Kaplan Publishing, 2002.

About the Authors

Michelle Le Patner is the Director of Research and Evaluation for Santa Ana Unified School District. In addition, she is a Professional Development Associate with The Leadership and Learning Center. Michelle has been a classroom teacher for students ranging from kindergarten through twelfth grade. She has worked with state boards of education, school districts, and Ministries and Departments of Education all around the world. The focus of her work is on the implementation of standards and assessment within the classroom setting.

Farid Matuk is a Peruvian-born poet, translator, and essayist. His honors include Ford and Fulbright Fellowships. He earned a Master in Fine Arts degree from the Michener Center for Writers at the University of Texas, Austin. He has worked as a bilingual educator and held a writer-in-the-schools post.

Literacy specialist **Rosemary Ruthven** has been in education since 1980, and has taught in both Australia and California. She was a curriculum specialist for the Santa Ana Unified School District in California and an adjunct professor for Chapman University, where she taught the teacher-training course "Literacy in the 21st Century." Rosemary has spoken at numerous national and international conferences on the components of a comprehensive literacy program. Currently, she consults and writes for school districts in both Australia and the United States.

Extraordinary Performance

The Leadership and Learning Center provides world-class professional development services, cutting-edge research, and innovative solutions for educators and school leaders who serve students from pre-kindergarten through college. The Center has worked in all fifty states and every Canadian province, as well as Europe, Africa, Asia, South America, and the Middle East. The Center works with public school systems, as well as religious and secular independent schools, charter schools, community colleges, technical schools, universities, state departments of education, national ministries of education, and international education associations. Center Professional Development Associates are experienced superintendents, principals, administrators, and educators who provide comprehensive practices for clients in the area of standards, assessment, instruction, accountability, data analysis, and leadership. If you would like to know more, please visit www.LeadandLearn.com or contact:

The
Leadership
and Learning
Center®

317 Inverness Way South, Suite 150, Englewood, CO 80112
866.399.6019 or 303.504.9312 | Fax 303.504.9417